Confession
Grea

The following confessions serve several purposes. The first is the renewing of your mind as you repeatedly hear yourself voice God's promises.

But then, as you purposefully choose to believe these truths, and as they become foremost in your thinking over what you have previously established in your mind, your speaking will begin to bring results.

This is how you turn the rudder of your ship. The rudder is your tongue; the ship is your life. James 3:4 & 5

These confessions are not necessarily meant to be prayers in the sense that you're asking God for these things, although, that is certainly okay. And don't think of them as only "positive confessions."

They are really meant to be a strong exercise of your authority as a representative of Heaven, to establish these promises and benefits in your world. Most of these things have already been ruled on and legally given to real Believers. It is our faith that brings them into being.

You may not even believe some of these things when you first begin, but the more you hear them (this is planting), the more they will become a part of you and overtake the garden of your mind. This was the meaning of the mustard seed that Jesus mentioned.

Jesus never said "faith the size of a mustard seed" would be enough for anything. That is a religious mistake created by translators who added the words "the size of," which are not part of the original text.

Jesus actually said, "If you have 'AS' a mustard seed, which is small, but then it grows to overtake the garden." Why would Jesus rebuke His men for "small faith," if small faith was enough? Seeds that don't "grow up," are useless. Mark 4:3-8

If you don't quit, the truth embedded in your words will begin to change your world as they leave your mouth and become established in the realm of the spirit. Faith filled words, coming out of your mouth in power, can work miracles in your life.

Words can become a hedge to protect you from evil as you speak the promises from Psalm 91. Demon spirits must bow to faith filled words. Your words can activate the holy angels of God that have been sent to serve and protect the heirs of salvation.
Hebrews 1:14.

Words can destroy diseases, just as Jesus' words destroyed the fig tree. Words can heal the sick and raise the dead when they're filled with faith. This could be your words if you'll plant the seeds.

When angels hear God's Word coming from your mouth, they will literally gather what you need in this life, or fight in your behalf. Let them hear you agreeing with, and saying, what the Bible promises.

Angels do not respond to the nonsense they often hear Christians saying. They most definitely respond to real faith based on the promises in the Word, though, WHEN THEY HEAR IT!

What are your angels hearing? Are they standing around waiting and waiting for you to finally say something that's filled with faith? Or do they cringe every time you exalt your problems over the Word?

You can start turning things around, today! Your mouth and your words are the Keys to the Kingdom. Keys represent "authority," and authority comes out of your mouth.

Words are containers. Fill them with faith. Jesus said, "My words are life." Your words can be life.

Faith must live in two places, "in your heart, and in your mouth." If it is only in your heart, there will be no authority released. If it is only in your mouth, but not in your heart, the mountain will not move for empty words.

Guns are used in natural warfare. But, in the spirit realm, your mouth is the weapon of choice.

Satan hates the authority we can wield over him with words. So, undoubtedly, you'll soon hear someone say: "Oh, that confession stuff doesn't really work, and words aren't really that important," or something similar.

Well, Jesus said we would be judged for every idle (non-productive) word. You would be wise to believe Jesus over anyone else, especially those who don't understand the reality of our authority.

When you don't get the Flu every year like they do, or worse, just smile and thank God for the same type of authority Jesus had. He never caught the flu, either.

Jesus never had to tell His disciples, "You boys go on to the Temple, I'm calling in sick today." Every disease known to man is under our feet, and every disease must bow to the Name of Jesus and our authority. Cancer does not scare God.

Don't expect a lot of help from others when you start speaking to mountains, or proclaiming your agreement with redemption. Usually, the opposite will come. But, this should let you know that what you're doing is working. Satan resists the truth.

Resistance can often be the first sign of success. Don't quit if things get worse. Just set yourself to be even more determined and fervent with your commands. Don't give Satan, or your problem(s), any choice whatsoever. You're the boss.

Jesus killed a tree with His words. He also stopped storms, ousted demons, destroyed diseases, and much more, all with His words. Why would it not work for us when He promised that it would? Your words are an exercise of your authority.

Always: Keep your eyes on the Word, and not on the problem. And, keep your mouth speaking the Word. Satan cannot stop you. Only you can.

How did Jesus know that the Roman Centurion had "great faith" in Matt. 8:10?

He **HEARD** it coming out of his mouth!

Boldly say the following. (Also, stop saying things that are contrary to these promises.) You will feel faith rise as you say and hear these things.

- According to Jesus' own words in Mark 11:23, I will have what I say if I believe. Therefore, I say these things believing that all of them are coming to pass in my life, daily. AMEN (so be it)!

- Jesus is the Son of God, the Christ, and I believe He is raised from the dead! Jesus is the Lord of my life, therefore, I am saved to the uttermost and I will never taste of eternal death.
Romans 10:8&9

- I am a new creation in Christ, old things are passed away and all things have become new, and they are given by God. I have the nature of God and the God kind of faith in me. As Jesus is, so am I in the earth. I am made in the image of God.
1 John 4:17

- The life and power of God are in me and greater is He that is in me, than he that is in the world.

- I am FULL of the Holy Spirit, FULL of love, FULL of boldness, and FULL of power. The anointing, fruits, and gifts operate I my life continuously.

- The love of God is shed abroad in my heart by the Holy Ghost. I am filled with love for God and people. I hate evil, but I love people and I forgive everyone who has wronged me.

D•   I am bone of Jesus' bone, and flesh of His flesh. I am reproduced just like Him and born of incorruptible seed, the Word. His blood has made me righteous and I am not just a mere man. I am strong in the power of His might, and quickened and raised up together with Him. Eph. 5:30 1 Peter 1:23

•   He has made me to sit in heavenly places with Him, FAR above ALL principality, power, might, and dominion, and above every name that is named in this world and the world to come. Eph. 2:6 Luke 10:19

•   All things are under my feet because they're under Jesus' feet and I'm part of His body, made in His image. As Jesus is, so am I in this earth. The works that He did, I do. I have the mind of Christ and I am His very righteousness, and I act accordingly. 2 Cor. 5:21   John 14:12

•   I only speak life to people. I never say a wrong word about anyone because they too are made in God's image. I speak no evil and I love everyone.

•   I am commissioned and sent. God is backing me for the Lord is on my side, as I am on His. What can man do unto me? I am an ambassador from Heaven. God never fails, and love never fails. God is love. Matt. 28:20

•	I am as bold as a lion because The Righteous are bold. I do not fear what people say or think. The Spirit of the Lord is upon me and I am endued with power from on high. Proverbs 28:1 Luke 4:18 Acts 1:8

•	I have been given power over ALL the power of the enemy, and nothing by any means shall hurt me or my family. I will preach the gospel, cast out devils, lay hands on the sick, and nothing can hurt me or my family, not even if we eat or drink any deadly thing. We are continuously healed by the stripes of Jesus. Luke 10:19 1 Peter 2:24

•	Every infectious germ, virus germ, and/or disease that touches my body, or any of my family's bodies, DIES INSTANTLY, in the Name of Jesus! The "Zoë" life of God flows through us, renewing us daily. Luke 10:19 Titus 3:5

•	Sickness and disease are repelled by the life of God in us, and by the Name of Jesus, and the authority given us through that Name, we have authority over all devils, diseases, and harmful things. Luke 10:17

•   Satan is eternally defeated and I have complete authority over him. I rule over circumstances and I am able through Christ to subdue. By faith, mountains must move before me according to the promise of Jesus. Mark 11:23

•   I am totally free from every unclean spirit. I command every demonic thing to leave me. I am totally free from hate, anger, worry, pride, fear, lust, jealousy, envy, depression, self-pity, legalism, and every evil influence.

•   Because Jesus has fulfilled the Law for me, and obeyed God's voice, all these blessings shall come on me, and overtake me…   Matt. 6:33

•   Blessed shall I be in the city, and blessed shall I be in the field.

•   Blessed shall be the fruit of my body, and the fruit of my ground, and the increase of my business and my wealth.

•   Blessed shall be my table and all my bank and financial accounts.

•   Blessed shall I be when I come in, and blessed shall I be when I go out.

I shall be the head only, and not the tail. I shall be above only, and not beneath.

• My family is totally free from every sin, pain, sickness, disease, sorrow, grief, infirmity, poverty, harm, debt, and condemnation. He who the Son sets free, is free indeed.

• I am full of faith, security, peace, love, wisdom, benevolence, joy, and the Holy Ghost. I don't spend time wallowing in negative emotions, or doubt and unbelief. I have power and control over these low things and they are beneath me. They do not rule over me.

• I choose to be happy today and every day. I am a happy person. I will not let circumstances or other people steal my joy and happiness. I insist on being happy, and I will enjoy life to the fullest.

• All of my days are blessed, for He daily loads me with benefits. Time is life, and my life is abundant in quality.   Psalm 68:19

• I thank you Lord for the angels that watch over us and protect us. They minister to us and for us bringing us all that we need. They surround us as the mountains surround Jerusalem, and they bear us up keeping us protected and safe from all danger and harm.   Psalm 91

- The Lord is my Shepherd and I shall not want. I shall not want for anything, including love, peace, health, faith, power, success, provision, safety, or any good thing. Psalm 23

- God has made Jesus unto me wisdom, righteousness, sanctification, and redemption. I am clean and righteous, and I ALWAYS know what to do in every situation. God is for me!   1 Cor. 1:30

- Confusion is always far from me, and I have been given a sound mind. The Holy Spirit is in me, helping my thoughts and giving me information as I need it. I am never at a loss for direction. 2 Tim. 1:7

- I have no care for I cast it all on the Lord and He cares for me. The battle is the Lord's and the victory is mine. My heart is fixed, and I will always praise the Lord. God is my sufficiency. 1 Peter 5:7

- God loves me as much as He loves Jesus. He is helping me think right thoughts. Lies and deception have no place in my being. I know the truth when I hear it, and all lies are exposed and gone from my thinking.   John 17:23

•   I know my calling and I hear God's voice clearly. I am extremely sensitive to the Holy Spirit. I am always tuned in to the Holy Spirit and I know what's going on in the spirit realm. I know when people are receiving and when they're not, and why, because I say so. Mark 11:23

•   I am a powerful minister for God. When I lay hands on the sick, they recover. Great signs and wonders follow me. I was made for signs and wonders. I am endued with power from on high. Favor compasses me like a shield. It is all around me, and on me. I have favor with God and men.

•   God leads me and guides me. He orders my footsteps and directs my path. I am always in the right place at the right time. God is bringing all that He has promised to pass. His sheep hear His voice, therefore, I hear His voice. He confirms His word in my life with signs following, as He promised.

•   I am full of energy and zeal, and I'm a success at all God leads me to put my hand to. My body will not fail even in old age. My vision is excellent and my teeth are strong and healthy.
Psalm 92:14

• 	Jesus is the Lord of my finances. He is my miracle worker, and my financial advisor. I ALWAYS make the right financial decisions. Jesus became poor to make me rich. He gave up His home so that could have one. He gave up all so that I could have all. I have been given power to get wealth. Psalm 32:8 2 Cor. 8:9 Deut. 8:18

• 	I will not criticize or complain. I have a thankful heart and a contrite spirit.

• 	My God supplies all my needs according to His riches in Glory by (because of) Christ Jesus. He will supply my needs even during a famine. I give and it is given back to me pressed down, shaken together, and running over. Our barns and savings accounts are filled with plenty. 2 Cor. 9:8

• 	Jesus is Lord over my entire life and I always have all the money I need to give away or use for my family. Due to Jesus, the windows of Heaven are always open on me, and they cannot be closed as long as I am in Him. They are pouring out blessings on me continuously. John 1:51

• 	I am free from any veil or blindness in my soul and understanding. I see clearly and anything that might keep me from seeing the truth is removed. My eyes and ears are always open to God.

• God has promised to lead me in the way I should go, and to teach me to profit, and I believe He is doing just that. Thank you Lord for all you do for me. Isaiah 48:17

• All of my bills are paid and debt is cast into the sea. We are completely and forever out of debt. Abundance and prosperity belongs to us because of Jesus. This is an absolute fact and benefit of my covenant with God.

• I have all sufficiency at all times to abound in every good work. We have land, housing, food, and clothing at all times, plus our bank accounts are full. Jesus has made us righteous and we are set in a large place. 2 Cor. 9:8

• The Holy Spirit shows me all truth and shows me things to come. He alerts me to financial opportunities and always warns me concerning any type of danger to me or my family. John 16:13

• The wealth of the sinner is reserved for the righteous, and I command wealth to come to me. I command money to come to me. I have wisdom and ideas for wealth. Wealth and riches shall be in my house, according to Psalm 112.

• I command Satan and every evil spirit of any rank or function to keep away from my finances, and to turn loose of money everywhere for the use of the Righteous. Satan cannot block my finances or anything else God has for me. Satan, you are under my feet and you have permission to do nothing but watch me get blessed!

• My family and all of my loved ones will be saved according to Acts chapter 16. My family will always walk with the Lord all the days of their lives. Satan has no power of influence over them because I have authority over him. My children will serve God and find His perfect will for their lives. My grandchildren and their children will also serve God.

• My marriage is successful and blessed. It is free from all strife and division. Jesus is Lord over all my relationships and they are all blessed of the Lord. My mate and I are one and Satan cannot come between us in any way.

• My family are believers, not doubters. The mystery of faith is in a pure conscience and we are the righteousness of God. My hands are Jesus' hands. When I lay hands on someone, Jesus is laying hands on them. My life is hidden in Christ.

- I never have a spirit of fear, but I do have one of love, power, and sound mind. I am full of boldness, confidence, and right thinking.

- Father, you promised to pour out your Spirit on all flesh, and you said I would prophesy, see visions, and do miracles. I thank you Lord that these things are happening in my life. Acts 2:17

- I ask you, Lord, to guard my tongue and keep me from saying anything I shouldn't. Let my conversation and my life always be pleasing to you. Keep me from hurting anyone, and keep me from harmful mistakes.

- Help me to be totally accurate in all the gifts of the Spirit, and I confess that very thing. Cause me to minister to people with efficiency and lasting results.

- Thank you Lord that these words carry your promises, and thank you for all that you have provided. I believe that these promises and words are coming to pass in my life even now, and always. Amen

Matthew 8:10
When Jesus heard it (the non-Jewish Centurion explaining authority), He marveled, and said to them that followed, "Truly, I say unto you, I have not found such great faith, no, not in Israel."

Understanding authority, which is exercised with words, is the key to possessing "Great Faith." Being apart from hindering, religious bondage, as this Centurion was, can also be helpful.

None of the Jews "under the law" had great faith. Jesus made this clear. This is a major insight into victory. Stay away from "The Law," or any subtle leaven of legalism. It will always hinder faith.

Matthew 8:26, And he said unto them, "Why are you fearful, O ye of little faith?" Then he arose, and rebuked the wind and the sea (with His words); and there was a great calm.

Matthew 9:2

And, behold, they brought to him a man sick of the palsy, lying on a bed: and Jesus seeing their faith said unto the sick of the palsy; "Son, be of good cheer; your sins are forgiven you."

Sin opened the door to sickness and disease. Hence, in God's mind, sin, disease, poverty, and all other by-products of sin, were thoroughly paid at the cross. There was no sickness or lack before there was sin. Jesus continuously demonstrated healing and provision in His ministry to make this point.

Matthew 9:22

But, Jesus turned about, and when He saw her He said, "Daughter, be of good comfort; your faith has made you whole." And the woman was made whole from that hour.

When this woman was healed, Jesus didn't even know who had touched Him, and still her faith produced the desired result. So, forget this religious idea that God has to rule "yes or no," to every healing request He receives. God has already ruled on healing, and the predetermined answer is "yes," according to II Cor. 1:20. The "stripes" on Jesus' back were for everyone, including you, and they were thorough.

Matthew 9:29
Then He touched their eyes, saying, "According to your faith, be it unto you."

Again and again, Jesus purposefully pointed out the faith of those who came to Him. He repeatedly said that they were healed because of their faith. It wasn't their performance or their good behavior that got results. It was their faith!

Matthew 15:28
Then Jesus answered and said unto her, "O woman, great is your faith: be it unto you even as you wish." And her daughter was made whole from that very hour.

This woman was not even a part of the Jewish people, or their covenant. But, she knew Jesus could help her. More than once, Jesus literally ignored her when she first came to Him. He then told her He was only sent to help the Jewish people, and not her.* Still, she persisted and He finally agreed, saying, "Woman, great is your faith."

Great faith doesn't take "no" for an answer. Never forget that, especially when someone is teaching on how God often denies our requests. Having faith can be a lonely experience in the church world.

*Jesus came to save everyone, but for legal reasons, He first had to present salvation to the Jews, due to His covenant with them. Then, after they rejected Jesus as their Messiah, salvation could be offered to the rest of the world along with the New Covenant. God thinks of everything.

Mark 10:52
And Jesus said unto him, "Go your way; your faith has made you whole." And immediately he received his sight and followed Jesus in the way.

Luke 9:41
And Jesus answering said, "O faithless and perverse generation, how long shall I be with you, and suffer you (allow or put up with)? Bring your son here."

Some of Jesus' own men didn't have the faith to cast out a devil. There are measures of faith, and varying measures of demonic strength. And, sometimes we just don't have enough faith. It is our responsibility to stay full and ready.

Obviously, Jesus was bothered that they didn't have the necessary faith, which is almost always the real answer for failed prayer. We like to make many other excuses, though. We even blame it on God with silly, religious reasoning. Authoritative faith is incredibly weak in most churches. You can help to change that.

Acts 3:16
And His name, through faith in His name, has made this man strong, whom you see and know: Yes, the faith which is by Him has given him this perfect soundness in the presence of you all.

Romans 1:17
For therein is the righteousness of God revealed from faith to faith: as it is written, "The just shall live by faith."

If you would like to know more about faith, order Bruce's book, "RUN TO THE GIANT."

Go to: RunToTheGiant.com

If you would like to have Bruce Wells speak at your church, group, or event, or, if you have a question or comment, email:

abrucewells@comcast.net

Gifts may be sent by check to: A. Bruce Wells
PO Box 972
Jensen Beach, FL 34958

Or through PayPal.com to
abrucewells@comcast.net

Made in the USA
Columbia, SC
16 February 2024

31640174R00017